3 0117 90119 1680

D0120578

SMALLEST

Ben H

A pygmy rattlesnake

CLASH

by **Tick** **Tock** **Books**

Publisher: Melissa Fairley
Art Director: Faith Booker
Editor: Victoria Garrard
Designer: Emma Randall
Production Controller: Ed Green
Production Manager: Suzy Kelly

ISBN: 978 1 84898 210 9

Copyright © *TickTock* Entertainment Ltd. 2010
First published in Great Britain in 2010 by *TickTock* Entertainment Ltd.,
The Old Sawmill, 103 Goods Station Road, Tunbridge Wells, Kent, TN1 2DP

Printed in China
1 3 5 7 9 10 8 6 4 2

A CIP catalogue record for this book is available from the British Library.
All rights reserved. No part of this publication may be reproduced, copied, stored in a retrieval
system or transmitted in any form or by any means electronic, mechanical, photocopying,
recording or otherwise without prior written permission of the copyright owner.

Picture credits (t=top; b=bottom; c=centre; l=left; r=right; OFC=outside front cover):
AFP/Getty Images: 5t, 18–19. Barry Bland/Barcroft Media Ltd: 22b. Andy Carter: 15c. Caters News Agency Ltd/Rex
Features: 27b, 29br. Mark Clifford/Barcroft Media Ltd: 5b, 20, 21, 29tr. Carl Court/PA Archive/Press Association Images:
2, 14–15, 28br. Courtesy of Robin Starr: 11, 28tr. Courtesy of The Arizona Aerospace Foundation: 10. Firebox.com: 4, 24,
29cl. Getty Images: 23. Motoring Picture Library/Alamy: OFC. NHPA/James Carmichael Jr: 1, 16–17, 29tl.
Ed Oudenaarden/epa/Corbis. Steven Schffner/Emporis: 6, 28tl. Shutterstock: 7, 13, 22t. South West News Service/
Rex Features: 16, 27tl. David Burner/Rex Features: 27tr. Takako Uno: 12, 29bl. Wildlife GmbH/Alamy: 8–9, 29cr.

Thank you to Lorraine Petersen and the members of nasen

Every effort has been made to trace copyright holders, and we apologize in advance for any omissions.
We would be pleased to insert the appropriate acknowledgements in any subsequent edition of this publication.

NOTE TO READERS
The website addresses are correct at the time of publishing. However, due to the ever-changing
nature of the internet, websites and content may change. Some websites can contain links that
are unsuitable for children. The publisher is not responsible for changes in content or website
addresses. We advise that internet searches should be supervised by an adult.

Peel P50

CONTENTS

The world we live in is getting bigger, but much of what we love is small. Small can be cool, clever and cute...

Actual size!

The smallest camcorder in the world is just 5.5 centimetres long.

The world's smallest helicopter can reach a speed of 100 kilometres an hour.

Mr Peebles is the world's smallest cat. He is the same size as a guinea pig.

Skyscrapers are the tallest buildings on Earth, but there is one that's surprisingly small.

The smallest skyscraper was built in Texas, USA, in 1919.

It's said that a con artist designed it. He told the people buying it that it would be 40 storeys high – instead it was only four! That's about 13 metres high.

The Vatican in Italy is the world's smallest country. It is home to the Pope.

It measures 0.44 square kilometres and has a population of around 900 people.

The Vatican has its own government, police force and even its own currency.

SMALLEST MAMMAL

The Etruscan pygmy shrew is the smallest mammal in the world.

It is 3.5 centimetres long, weighs 1.8 grams and has a life span of 15 months.

Because it is so small the shrew has to eat constantly to stay warm. It eats insects and spiders, which it kills with its poisonous bite.

SMALLEST PLANE

The smallest plane in the world was called Bumblebee II.

In 1984 Robert Starr built the Bumblebee to set the record for the smallest plane. But the record was soon broken by another plane, so Robert built the Bumblebee II in 1988.

Bumblebee

However, on its first flight, Bumblebee II crashed! Robert was OK, but the plane was destroyed. Luckily, he had flown Bumblebee II for enough time to set a new record.

Bumblebee II stats
- Length: 2.7 metres
- Weight: 179.6 kilograms
- Wingspan: 1.7 metres
- Top speed: 305 kilometres per hour

Bumblebee II

SMALLEST SEAHORSE

Satomi's pygmy seahorse is only the size of your fingernail.

At 13 millimetres long it is the smallest seahorse in the world.

As with all seahorses, it is the males that give birth, not the females.

Same size as a fingernail

Satomi's seahorses give birth to a baby the size of a comma!

Seahorses vary greatly in size. The biggest can be up to 30 centimetres long.

SMALLEST CAR

The *Peel P50* is the smallest car ever made.

The Peel P50 *parked in Piccadilly Circus, London.*

It is designed to fit only one person. The car is 1.2 metres high and 1.3 metres long.

The *Peel P50* has no reverse gear. The driver has to get out of the car and use a special handle to lift the car up and turn it.

Handle to lift the car up and turn it.

The *Peel*'s top speed is just 64 kilometres per hour.

SMALLEST RATTLESNAKE

The pygmy rattlesnake is only 45 centimetres long, but it often bites people.

It uses its fangs to inject venom into its prey. Although not deadly to humans, its bite can make us very ill.

Leaf

All rattlesnakes have a rattle at the end of their tail. The pygmy's rattle is so small it sounds more like a soft 'buzz'.

Rattle

SMALLEST HELICOPTER

Have you ever wished you could travel to school in a personal helicopter?

The GEN H-4 could be for you!

The GEN H-4 is the smallest manned helicopter in the world. It weighs 70 kilograms and has a top speed of 100 kilometres an hour. From top to bottom it measures just 2.4 metres.

It has two rotors, a chair, a footrest and a handlebar. The handlebar makes you go forwards, backwards, left or right.

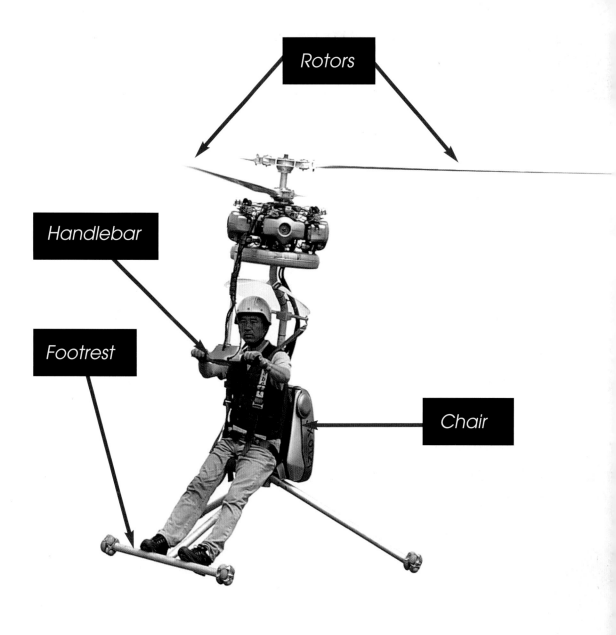

Rotors

Handlebar

Footrest

Chair

Just strap in and you're ready to go!

SMALLEST PET CAT

The smallest pet cat in the world is called Mr Peebles.

At only 15 centimetres long and weighing 1.4 kilograms, Mr Peebles can fit into a small glass.

A vet first noticed the cat during a visit to a farm. Everyone thought Mr Peebles was just a kitten.

But on closer inspection the vet realized Mr Peebles was a fully-grown cat!

Despite his size, Mr Peebles eats four meals a day.

Roborovski is the smallest type of hamster. They grow to just five centimetres long.

Heaven Sent Brandy, a chihuahua, is the smallest living dog. She is just 15.2 centimetres from nose to tail.

Thumbelina is the smallest living horse. She is 44.5 centimetres high.

SMALLEST CAMERA

Have you ever dreamed of becoming the next James Bond? Or perhaps a movie director?

The smallest camcorder in the world will come in handy for either.

Record button

Actual size!

The Muvi Micro Camcorder is only 5.5. centimetres long, weighs 50 grams and is small enough to hang around your neck.

The camera certainly isn't complicated to use. It only has one button – record.

The DelFly Micro is a tiny remote-controlled plane with a camera. It has a wingspan of just ten centimetres. It's in the Guinness Book of Records as the smallest camera plane.

The plane has a tiny battery on board which powers the plane for up to three minutes. Because of its size, the DelFly Micro can be used to take photos of difficult-to-reach or dangerous places.

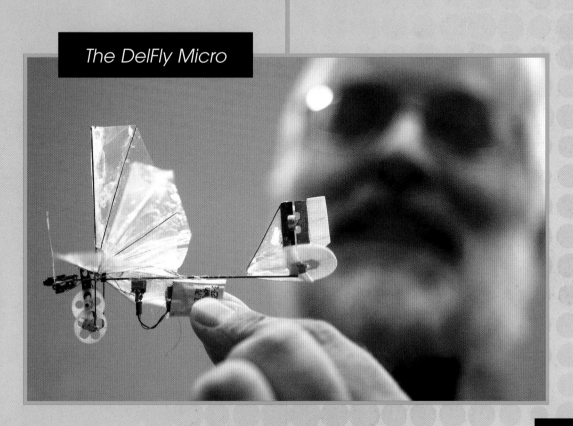

The DelFly Micro

SMALLEST SCULPTURES

Willard Wigan makes sculptures so small you need a microscope to see them.

The sculptures fit onto the head of a pin, or into the eye of a needle.

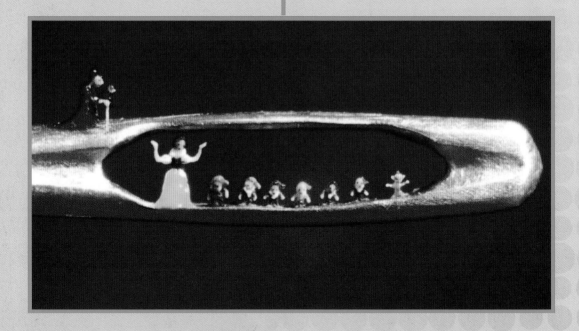

Willard has used an eyelash and even a grain of sand to make his sculptures.

He says the hardest part is staying still enough to work.

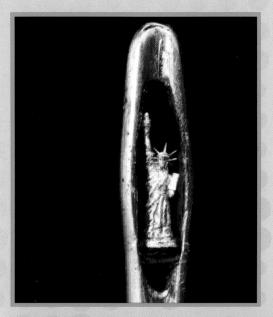
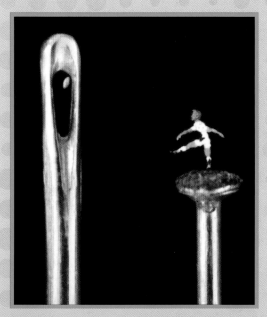

**"Every movement I make is so small.
I have to control my breathing and
heartbeat, it's not easy."**
Willard Wigan

TOP TEN SMALLEST

Some of the smallest things on Earth are created by nature.

Others were built by humans.

They are all amazing record breakers.

10

Smallest skyscraper:

LaSalle Street, Wichita Falls, USA, 13 metres high

9

Smallest plane:

Bumblebee II, 2.7 metres long

8

Smallest helicopter:

GEN H-4, 2.4 metres high

7

Smallest car:

Peel P50, 1.3 metres long

6

Smallest rattlesnake:

Pygmy rattlesnake,
45 centimetres long

5

Smallest pet cat:

Mr Peebles,
15 centimetres long

4

Smallest camera:

Muvi Micro Camcorder,
5.5 centimetres long

3

Smallest mammal:

Etruscan pygmy shrew,
3.5 centimetres long

2

Smallest seahorse:

Satomi's pygmy seahorse,
13 millimetres long

1

Smallest sculptures:

Willard Wigan's,
0.005 millimetres

NEED TO KNOW WORDS

camcorder
A lightweight, hand-held videocassette recorder.

con artist Someone who cheats or tricks people by persuading them something is true, when it is not.

Guinness World Records
An organization that records and measures record-breaking things and events. The world records are then published in a book each year.

lifespan The length of time a human or animal lives for.

mammal An animal with fur or hair that gives birth to a live baby and feeds it with milk from its own body. A mammal's body temperature stays the same no matter how hot or cold the air or water is around it.

manned When a human is on board or on site.

rattle Quick knocking sounds, or anything that makes a rattle sound.

remote-controlled
A device that is operated without the use of wires and from a distance.

sculpture Art that is made in 3D, often carved out of stone, wood or cast from metal or plaster.

skyscraper A very tall building that tends to dominate a skyline.

venom A powerful poison produced in the bodies of some animals, such as snakes, and spiders.

wingspan
A measurement of the tip of one wing to the tip of the other.

SMALL FACTS

- The dwarf lantern shark is around 16 centimetres long. You could hold it in your hand, so it's reasonably harmless.

- Bonsai is the Japanese art of growing miniature trees. The smallest bonsais are called Keshi-tsubu and are less than 2.5 centimetres high.

- The smallest house in the world is in Amsterdam, Holland. It is just one metre wide.

FIND OUT MORE ONLINE...

http://www.guinnessworldrecords.com

http://www.mydigitallife.info/2009/06/13/the-worlds-smallest-dv-camera-muvi-micro-dv-cam/

http://www.peel-cars-p50.co.uk/

http://www.willard-wigan.com/

http://www.worldssmallesthorse.com/

INDEX